But Columbus knew the world was round.
He thought he could reach Japan by sailing West.
He didn't know there was any land in between.

Columbus needed money to pay for ships and a crew. It was difficult to get people to believe in his plan. Many sailors were too frightened to sail across the open sea.

Oxford Primary History

Christopher Columbus

A famous explorer

Tim Vicary

Oxford University Press 1993

Christopher Columbus was a sailor from Italy.
Sailing was very difficult in those days.
Sailors didn't like to sail far from the coast.
Some people even believed the world was flat.

Kings and Queens who had money wouldn't listen to him. He said 'I will come back with a lot of gold. You will be rich.'

At last, the King and Queen of Spain gave him three small ships.

They were called the *Nina*, the *Pinta*, and the *Santa Maria*.

In August 1492, Columbus landed on the Canary islands.
People there said, 'Yes, we think there is land to the west.'
Columbus was pleased, and sailed on.
There were no more islands. Just wide empty sea.

The sailors on the *Nina* said: 'Look! Land – over there!' They sailed towards it, but it was only clouds, not land.

One day, he saw seaweed, floating round the ships. There were little white crabs on the seaweed, and Columbus caught one.

'Crabs don't go far from land,' he said. 'We must be nearly there.'

After a month at sea, the sailors were getting fed up.

'We'll go on for three more days,' they said.
'Then we'll throw Columbus in the sea and go home.'

One night, they saw a light shining between the waves.
'It's land!' Columbus said happily.
'It's the moon shining on a white beach!'
The sailors sang and thanked God.

Next morning they went on shore.
The island was full of fruit and fresh water.
Columbus put up a Spanish flag on the beach.

'This land belongs to the King of Spain now,' he said.
The people of the island came to talk to Columbus.
They gave him cotton and parrots.
Columbus gave them beads and bells.

Columbus sailed to a bigger island called Haiti.
He thought it was Japan.

The people came to his ships in big canoes.
They gave him bread and fish and water and gold.
'These are very kind people,' Columbus said.
'They give us everything we want.'

One night, in a storm, the *Santa Maria* was blown onto rocks and sank.
The sailors were saved, but there were only two ships left now.

Columbus spoke to his men.
'I can't take you all home,' he said.
'Some of you will have to stay here.'
Forty men stayed behind.
'I'll come back for you next year,' Columbus promised.

The *Nina* and the *Pinta* sailed on through terrible storms.
Waves crashed right over the ship.
'Please God, save us!' the sailors cried. 'Don't let us die!'

Some people from the islands were on the ships too.
They were frightened and unhappy.
They didn't want to be taken to Spain.
They wanted to go back to their islands.

When they reached Spain, Columbus went to see the King and Queen.
He showed them the gold and the people from the islands.
'I have sailed to Japan!' he said proudly.

The King and Queen were very pleased.
'Go back, with these letters to the King of Japan!' they said.
So Columbus sailed off again, this time with seventeen ships.

When they reached the islands again, the Spanish sailors built towns and dug for gold.
They made the people of the islands work so hard that most of them died.

Columbus never found the King of Japan,
because he was in the wrong place.
The islands were really only half way to Japan.
Columbus didn't know it, but he had found a New World.
Today, we call it America.

Timeline for Christopher Columbus

No one knows when Columbus was born. Some people think he was born in 1436, other people say 1451.

April 1492	The King and Queen of Spain give Columbus 3 ships.
August 1492	Columbus starts his voyage.
September 1492	They see the clouds and crabs and seaweed.
October 1492	The sailors see land.
January 1493	Columbus sails home.
March 1493	Columbus reaches Spain.
1493–1496	Columbus' second voyage.
1498–1500	Columbus' third voyage.
1502–1504	Columbus' fourth voyage.
20 May 1505	Columbus dies.

Oxford University Press, Walton Street, Oxford OX2 6DP

Oxford New York Toronto
Delhi Bombay Calcutta Madras Karachi
Kuala Lumpur Singapore Hong Kong Tokyo
Nairobi Dar es Salaam Cape Town
Melbourne Auckland Madrid

and associated companies in
Berlin Ibadan

Illustrations by Tony James Chance

First published 1993
Reprinted 1993

0 19 917231 5
0 19 917241 2 (pack of 6)

Typeset by Pentacor PLC, High Wycombe, Bucks
Printed in Hong Kong